This Book Belongs To:

This book and its content is copyright of ItsjustJax Productions

©2022 ItsjustJax Productions. All rights reserved.

Any redistribution or reproduction of part or all of the contents in any form is prohibited other than the following:

- You may copy the content to individual third parties for their personal use, but only if you acknowledge the book as the source of the material.

Written permission must be attained by the publisher,
To distribute or commercially use content.

Helpful Hint

The sentence on the scroll is called a pangram. What makes it helpful is that it contains every letter of the alphabet. When the writer completes all the lessons, this reduces practice time to repeating this one simple sentence. An extra bonus is once the sentence is learned, it will be the only thing needed to recall the skill from memory.

Helpful Stuff

Want a fun way to read cursive?

Crack the Cursive Code is also available as a full-color adventure story book written in cursive complete with printed version for translation in the back of the book.

Love to listen to audiobooks?

Hear the almost 3000 word story of Crack the Cursive Code in the half hour long audiobook version. Play along with the story book or activity book to increase the fun and learning potential!

These and more can be found at
www.crackthecursivecode.com

b Helpful

Two b's or not two b's.
It was brought to my attention that the original lowercase "b" in this book was written in a contemporary format since the traditional cursive lowercase "b" never had a little loop on its finishing stroke. Both formats are included.

One afternoon, Dog was woken from a nap by two friends,
Fox and Chicken. "Let's play dress up!" clucked Chicken.
"Pick a costume from this trunk." Fox was fastest and dressed as a spy.
"The name's Hunt... Eat N. Hunt," said Fox, fixing a false moustache into place.
Next, the chicken found a wizard's robe and wand.
"Magical stories are my favorite, so I'm the Lord of the Wings."
The sleepy dog was slowest and chose an explorer's outfit.
It had a whip and an old-fashioned hat called a fedora.
"You can call me Indie 'Napper' Bones," barked Dog.
Then, Wings pulled out an old scroll from the wizard's cloak.
"Look what I've found!" clucked the chicken, unrolling the scroll.
Bones, Hunt, and Wings stared at the curly writing on the cracked paper.
None of them could read what the strange writing said.
"It looks like an ancient language," said Hunt.
"Only a super spy can crack this code!"

"It could be a magic spell," warned Wings. "I think we should be careful." Bones whirled the explorer's whip acrobatically in the air. "There's no need to be anxious at all! I've actually picked up the aroma of an absolutely amazing adventure!"

Wings' wand began to glow. Moving without any assistance, it wrote the outline of a letter "a" in the air.

POOF!

The three friends were no longer in the backyard. They were standing on the deck of a ship! A big, blue wave blatantly blasted Hunt in the face. "I spy we're sailing on the sea," said the soggy fox. "This is brilliant!" barked Bones, who was bouncing toward the bow. "We're on a big, beautiful, and buoyant boat."

The magic wand burst into life again and drew a letter "b" in the air.

traditional

contemporary

trace the letters and words for practice

A a

a a a a a a a a a a a a

A a A a A a

Air   air

amazing

B b b

b b b b b b b b b b b

B b B b B b

Brown

brilliant

Wings was concerned by the choppy sea water. The cowering chicken tried to keep the cracked paper dry. "Why don't you come inside?" asked a voice. It was… a crocodile! Cautious of the crocodile's considerable claws, the three companions followed the scaly creature to the ship's bridge.

Hovering in the cabin, the magic wand carefully wrote a curly "c".

"I'm James T. Croc, celebrated captain and cartographer," said the crocodile, clasping the ship's wheel. "Welcome to my boat! From here I control my cruising craft."

"Thanks, Captain," said Hunt. "It's cool to come aboard."

The glowing wand danced through the room, drawing a letter "d" as it did so.

"Do you have a desired direction of travel?" asked the captain. "No," replied Wings. "We're on a quest to decode this scroll. My wand dropped us onto your deck, but we don't know why it decided to do that." Croc smiled. The captain's pointy teeth were a dramatic dental display. "The wand directed you here because this little dinghy is the darndest, most diverse ship on the seven seas. It can take us anywhere." The captain dragged a lever down and a loud DING DING rang out on every deck. "We will dive down to the depths," said the captain, "and discover your destination."

trace the letters and words for practice *Cc*

cccccccccccccccc

Cc Cc Cc

Cool   cool

crocodile

Dd

dddddddddddd

Dd Dd Dd

Dog   dog

discover

The friends did not expect what happened next.
The boat transformed into a submarine and sank to the bottom of the sea!
Then, there was an extremely loud CLANG which echoed everywhere and the emergency lights flashed an eerie red.
"We've been trapped by an electric eel!" exclaimed Captain Croc. "Even my exceptional engineer estimates we won't ever escape."

The magic wand exploded into action again and drew a glowing letter "e" in the air.

As fast as lightning, Hunt flew from the room.
A few fearful moments followed, then finally the furry fox reappeared, squeezing water from his soaking fur. "You've got nothing to fear," said Hunt. "I'm the fastest fox there is. I swam outside and faced the fearsome eel, who couldn't fight me and fled."

The fantastic wand floated across the cabin, forming the outline of a letter "f".

trace the letters and words for practice. **E e**

eeeeeeeeeeeeeeeeee

E e E e E e

Eel   eel

electric

F f

f f f f f f f f f f f

F f F f F f

Fox   fox

furry

The underwater boat gracefully glided toward the sun that glistened on the ocean's surface. Wings was grateful to be greeted by the sky and a few gulls. Getting in a submarine was like being trapped in a soup can! Gathered on the gleaming gray roof, the captain thanked the gallant Hunt. "You saved us." Captain Croc grinned.

"I wish I had a gorgeous gift to give you. Instead, to show my gratitude, I will transform this submarine again. It will guide us to greater places."

The wand began to glow and wrote a glinting letter "g" in the air.

Then, the weary hound heaved himself out of the highest hatch and onto the top of the submarine. "All this hurling around makes my eyelids heavy," yawned Bones. "Here's a handsome spot to have a heavenly half-hour nap." The dog hastily hung a hammock and had his head down in hardly any time at all! Hunt had had enough.

"Having a nap is hardly helpful! We're in a hurry over here. You really put the zzzzzzz in lazy hound." Captain Croc smiled. "He won't sleep for long. Be ready to hop into your new hot air balloon!"

The wand hovered into the air again, drawing the shape of a letter "h".

trace the letters and words for practice Gg

g g g g g g g g g g

G g G g G g

Gift   gift

gorgeous

Hh

h h h h h h h h h h

H h H h H h

Hop   hop

hound

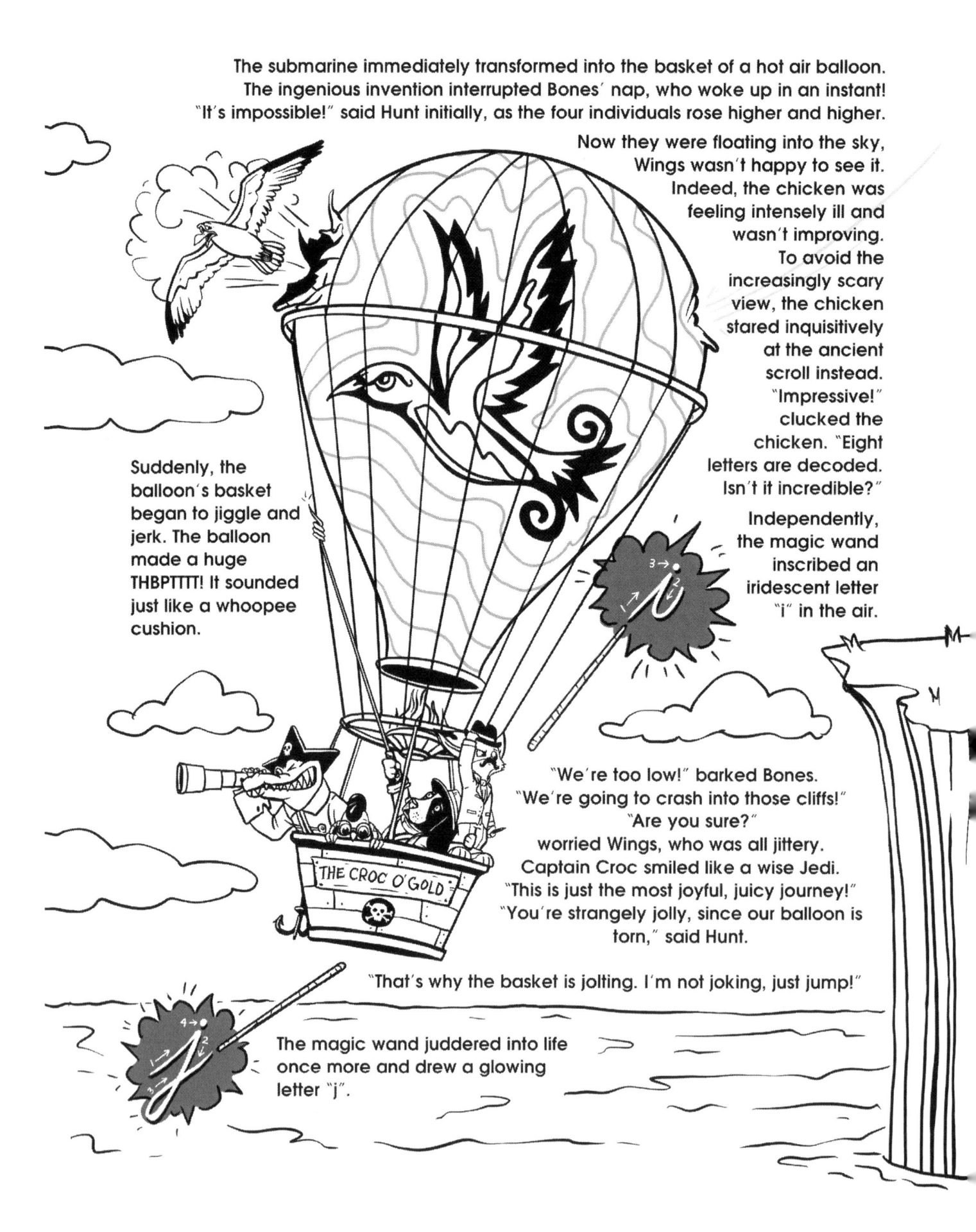

The submarine immediately transformed into the basket of a hot air balloon. The ingenious invention interrupted Bones' nap, who woke up in an instant! "It's impossible!" said Hunt initially, as the four individuals rose higher and higher.

Now they were floating into the sky, Wings wasn't happy to see it. Indeed, the chicken was feeling intensely ill and wasn't improving. To avoid the increasingly scary view, the chicken stared inquisitively at the ancient scroll instead. "Impressive!" clucked the chicken. "Eight letters are decoded. Isn't it incredible?"

Suddenly, the balloon's basket began to jiggle and jerk. The balloon made a huge THBPTTTT! It sounded just like a whoopee cushion.

Independently, the magic wand inscribed an iridescent letter "i" in the air.

"We're too low!" barked Bones. "We're going to crash into those cliffs!"
"Are you sure?" worried Wings, who was all jittery.
Captain Croc smiled like a wise Jedi.
"This is just the most joyful, juicy journey!"
"You're strangely jolly, since our balloon is torn," said Hunt.

"That's why the basket is jolting. I'm not joking, just jump!"

The magic wand juddered into life once more and drew a glowing letter "j".

trace the letters and words for practice.   *I i*

i i i i i i i i i i i i i i i i i i i

I i   I i   I i

Into   into

incredible

J j

j j j j j j j j j j j j j j j j j j

J j   J j   J j

Jump   jump

journey

The off-kilter basket dropped from the sky.
It landed with a KA-RUMP at the bottom of the rocky cliffs.
Bones and Wings also landed on their bottoms.
The flat balloon flopped on top of them like a big red pancake.
"We weren't killed? You're kidding me!" said Bones.
The dog came out kicking from under the burst balloon.
Then, Bones spotted the kooky crocodile, who was floating into the distance.
"Keep on with your quest!" shouted Captain Croc, blowing a kiss.
The captain's jacket had turned into a kite!

"Well, the kindly Captain Croc kept that a secret," said Bones. "I'm keen to go back to my kennel."

The kinetic wand flew into the air again, drawing the shape of a letter "k".

Hunt leaped out from the limp, lifeless balloon without a single hair out of place. The lucky fox had landed feet first, as spies always do.
"You can't leave," lectured Hunt. "That's the lazy way out. Look! There's a large ladder leaning against the looming cliffs. It might lead us to the next letter."

The magic wand lifted itself off the beach, writing the latest letter "l" in the air.

trace the letters and words for practice.   K k

k k k k k k k k k k k k

K k K k K k

Kiss   kiss

kooky

L l

l l l l l l l l l l l l

L l L l L l

Lazy   lazy

lucky

The motivated fox moved quickly and motored up the ladder.
The chicken minced afterwards, mighty glad of making it back to dry land.
The tired pooch meandered across the beach and mounted the ladder last.
At the top of the cliff was a marvelous green field. In the distance they could just make out...

"A mountain!" said Hunt, twitching his fake moustache. "We must move! The magic wand wants us to march across this massive meadow and make our way toward the mountain. That must be our mission."

The magic wand moved through the air, marking the sparkling outline of a letter "m".

Hunt dashed off, navigating noiselessly through the grass.
The near-sighted Wings looked at the large meadow.
Free-range spaces made the chicken very nauseous.

"That's our mission?" gulped Wings. "Not possible."
Now, Bones noticed that Wings was nickering.
"There's no need to be nervous, it's just nature," said the dog.
"Plus, I've got a good nose. I'll navigate us across no problem."

The magic wand hovered again, drawing a new glowing shape, the letter "n".

trace the letters and words for practice. **M m**

m m m m m m m m

M m M m M m

March   march

marvelous

N n

n n n n n n n n

N n N n N n

Nose   nose

navigate

Bones led Wings to the opposite side of the meadow, using the whip to open a path through the oversized grass. They found Hunt relaxing at the bottom of the mountain. He was occupying a sofa... an orange blow-up sofa!

"Where did that come from?" asked Wings in an outburst.

"From this opulent pen!" replied Hunt. The fox clicked on the end of the pen. The orange sofa was sucked back inside it! "A good spy always has gadgets for official operations," offered Hunt. "A better spy knows when to use them," barked Bones, offended. "In my opinion, it's obvious we could have landed on that earlier, instead of our bottoms!"

"Oh well." The fox smirked. "I hope your outdoor ordeal wasn't too odious. Now, it's obvious we should go onward to obtain our objective." "What?" asked the confused chicken. "Our only option," said Hunt. "Over the mountain!"

The glowing wand wrote the outline of a letter "o" in the air.

A rocky trail twisted around the side of the mountain. As the pals proceeded, the steeper the punishing path became. Large portions were particularly poor, where the sides of the narrow track were crumbling. Petrified of plunging to a poultry end, Wings clung to Bones. Plenty of loose pebbles and rocks plummeted far below them. Refreshed from the earlier rest, a perky Hunt pursued the path much faster than his pals.

"Please keep up with my pace," said the puzzled fox, "or I'll have to push you up the path. It really isn't that perilous."

As they progressed, the magic wand floated above the path, drawing a perfect letter "p".

trace the letters and words for practice.

O o

o o o o o o o o o o o o o o o o

O o O o O o

Over over

outdoor

P p

p p p p p p p p p p

P p P p P p

Pals pals

puzzled

Wings didn't want to see how high the quarreling friends were climbing. The quivering chicken opened the scroll again.

"Look! Sixteen letters are now decoded."

Suddenly, Wings tripped and nearly fell over the edge! Bones grabbed the chicken's wing just in time. "I know I can be lazy," quipped the dog, "but I've got quality instincts." Bones helped Wings back onto the path. The dog barked a question to the speedy fox ahead. "Can you slow down, Hunt?"

"Quiet!" said the fox. "Move quicker and quit quibbling."

The magic wand spun through the air quite quaintly drawing a glowing letter "q".

Hunt raced off rapidly into the distance.

"Thanks Bones," clucked Wings, relieved.

"I really wish my wand could return us home."

"I know," replied Bones. "But it wants us to solve the riddle of the ancient letters."

The dog looked up their rugged route and saw the fox's retreating brown tail. It was almost out of range, just visible through a cloud of dust on the rising, rubbled ramp! "I'd better run up this risky, rocky road. That rascal Hunt is really rocketing now."

The magic wand rose upward and wrote the outline of a letter "r" in the air.

trace the letters and words for practice.

Qq

q q q q q q q q q q q q

Q q Q q Q q

Quick   quick

question

Rr

n n n n n n n n n n n n

R n R n R n

Rocky   rocky

riddle

As Bones spied Hunt, the dog's nostrils sniffed a new scent. The smell of a new creature was suspended in the air. Something that was deadly for sure! The surprised hound strode after the stubborn fox with every ounce of strength. Bones caught up with Hunt and stopped the speeding fox from surging up the slope.

"Stop!" shouted Bones. "Don't step any further!"

The brown fox jumped over the dog. "Don't be so lazy." The springing Hunt scowled. The sure-footed fox landed on a patch of leaves… and suddenly sank out of sight! The leaves had been spread over a substantial hole in the surface of the path. From the hole, Bones could hear the sound of a sinister hisssss.

"Save me!" shouted a scared Hunt.

"I'm stuck in a snake pit. The slippery serpents are swarming and snapping at me."

Silently, the magic wand soared skyward as it drew the shape of a sparkling letter "s".

The trusty dog leaped to the edge of the terrifying hole. Down below, the tense fox was trying to twist away from the teeming tangle of snakes. Bones twirled the explorer's whip and tumbled it into the snake trap. A tearful Hunt took hold of the taut whip. "Trust me," barked Bones. "It's time to teach those toxic terrors they can't take a bite!"

The glowing wand travelled through the air and wrote the outline of a letter "t".

trace the letters and words for practice.

Ss

s s s s s s s s s s s s s s s s s s

S s S s S s

Snake   snake

surprised

Tt

t t t t t t t t t t t t t t t

T t T t T t

Time   time

Twirled

The unbelievable dog pulled the unusually uneasy fox from the unimaginably awful hole. Both animals lay on the path, panting in unison from the undertaking.
"I should have listened to you," said Hunt, "instead of unfairly urging us ahead."
The shaken fox stirred and helped the unselfish dog stand up.
"Thanks to you, I'm unhurt. I understand if you're upset. I was unreasonable and unkind as we came uphill."

By itself, the glowing wand floated upward, drawing a letter "u" in the air.

Wings arrived too late to see the valiant rescue from the vicious snakes.
"This valuable wand has written five more letters," said the chicken. "What did I miss?"
Voluntarily, Hunt told Wings a vivid version of Bones' virtuous efforts, despite the fox's vanity. Soon, the three friends were victorious in reaching the top of the mountain vista. The verdant landscape was visible for miles and miles!
"Where do we venture next?" asked Wings.
"I'm not leading," said Hunt the humbled vulpine.
"It's time I stopped being vocal and listened to someone else."
"We're close to our goal..." barked Bones, "very close. In my view, we should veer this way and into this valley."

The magic wand wrote the outline of a vibrant letter "v" in the air.

trace the letters and words for practice. 𝒰 u

u u u u u u u u u u u u

U u U u U u

Up up Up

unison

𝒱 v

v v v v v v v v v v v

V v V v V v

Vivid vivid

valuable

"We've had quite a journey to get here," yawned Bones.
"I'm sure you have," said the wizard. "As you wandered yonder, yearning for home, what wisdom did your journey yield? What did you learn?"

"Though my beak may be yellow... I can still be brave," replied Wings.
"Even though I yelled at them," said Hunt, "these two still want to be my friends."

"Oh yes," the wizard replied.
"You young ones will be friends for years."

Wings' wand glowed again and, yawing in the air, wrote the shape of a letter "y".

"Look!" said the wizard. "There's only one letter left." This time, it was the wizard's wand that glowed. Hunt and Wings watched in amazement as it zoomed in a zigzag across the room.

As it flew, it drew the glowing outline of a letter "z".

"I don't understand," said the fox, confused.
"Nobody said that letter."
"Zzzzzzzzz..."
Hunt and Wings turned around.
Curled in a corner of the cave, Bones was SNORING!

trace the letters and words for practice. Y y

y y y y y y y y y y

Y y Y y Y y

Yawn yawn

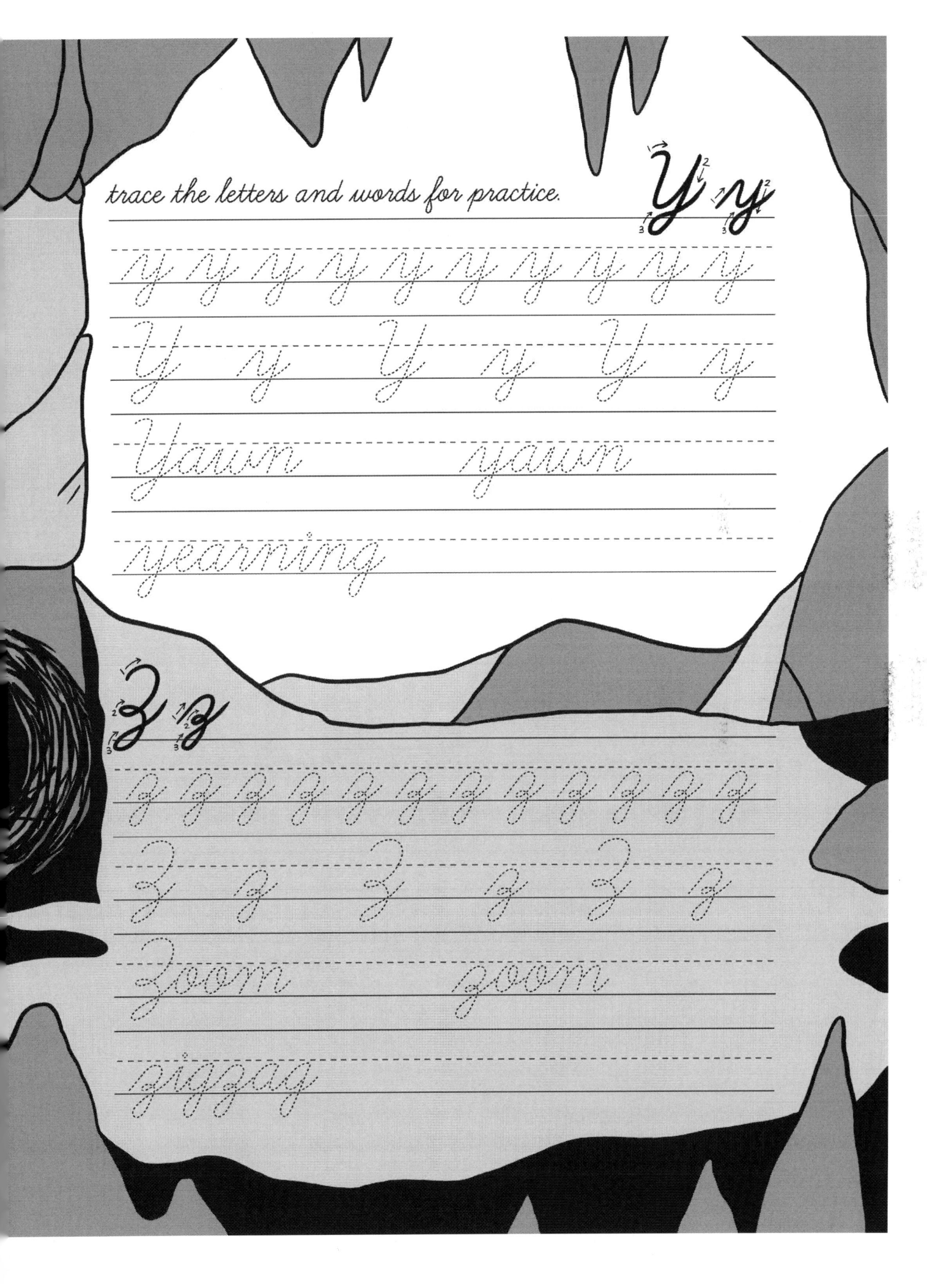

yearning

Z z

z z z z z z z z z z

Z z Z z Z z

zoom zoom

zigzag

The wizard spread the scroll on the stony cave floor.
Finally, Hunt and Wings could read the sentence they had decoded.

The quick brown fox jumps over the lazy dog.

The wizard ruffled his feathers proudly.
"Congratulations," hooted the owl. "This sentence contains all the letters
of the alphabet. It will help you to decipher any future code."
"What does it mean?" asked Wings.
"I called Bones lazy," said Hunt, "and jumped into the snake pit.
Sometimes it's good to be quick, but sometimes it's good to take your
time... and not leave others behind."

"That's right," came a bark from behind them.
Bones was awake!
"I can be lazy," said the dog, "and I do get very tired. But sometimes I'm slow
because my nose tells me to be cautious." Bones put his paws on Wings' and
Hunt's shoulders. "And I'll always be ready to spring into action for my friends."
The wizard smiled his biggest smile yet.
"You are very wise," he said,
"just like the people who used this old cursive handwriting. In writing like this, all
the letters join together. Just as you have joined together to decipher this
manuscript. Along the way you learned to work as a team, which makes this
scroll even more valuable."

The owl wizard waved his wand and magic
shimmered around the three friends.

"Why not practice this writing together...
when you get home."

The quick brown
The quick brown
fox jumps over
fox jumps over
the lazy dog.
the lazy dog.

POOF

The three friends were back by the kennel in the yard.
They still wore their costumes and the chicken still had the scroll.
The only thing missing was the magic wand.
"Well," barked Dog, "I guess we're just plain old Dog, Fox, and Chicken again."
"Maybe," clucked Chicken. "But now we know this magical writing, things might never be the same again."
"That's right." Fox grinned. "One day soon, Bones, Hunt, and Wings will have another absolutely amazing adventure."

Join the

Cursive CREW

in their next adventure:

I before E conspiracy

CRACK the Cursive CODE
By Jax

CRACK the Cursive CODE

BY Jax

Lord of the Wings

Lord of the Wings

India "Napper" Bones

India "Napper" Bones

Eat N. Hunt

Eat N. Hunt

Eat N. Hunt

Aa	Bb	Cc	Dd
Ee	Ff	Gg	Hh
Ii	Jj	Kk	Ll
Mm	Nn	Oo	Pp
Qq	Rr	Ss	Tt
Uu	Vv	Ww	Xx
	Yy	Zz	

Wise Wizard & Captain Croc

trace the letters and words for practice   **Aa**

a a a a a a a a a a a a a a

A a A a A a

Air air

amazing

Bbb

b b b b b b b b b b b b b b

B b B b B b

Brown

brilliant

𝒶 𝒶 𝒶 𝒶 𝒶 𝒶 𝒶 𝒶 𝒶 𝒶

𝒶 𝒶 𝒶 𝒶 𝒶

𝒶 𝒶 𝒶 𝒶 𝒶 𝒶 𝒶 𝒶 𝒶 𝒶 𝒶

𝒶 𝒶 𝒶 𝒶 𝒶

Boat   Anchor   bird

ℬ ℬ ℬ ℬ ℬ

𝒷 𝒷 𝒷 𝒷 𝒷 𝒷 𝒷 𝒷 𝒷 𝒷 𝒷 𝒷

𝒷 𝒷 𝒷 𝒷 𝒷

𝒷 𝒷 𝒷 𝒷 𝒷

Practice!

CRACK the Cursive CODE

Connectors

aa ab ac ad ae

af ag ah ai aj

a

ak al am an ao

ap aq ar as at au

av aw ax ay az

Practice!

Connectors

b

ba bb bc bd be

bf bg bh bi bj

bk bl bm bn bo

bp bq br bs bt bu

bv bw bx by bz

Practice!

Connectors

b

ba bb bc bd be

bf bg bh bi bj

bk bl bm bn bo

bp bq br bs bt bu

bv bw bx by bz

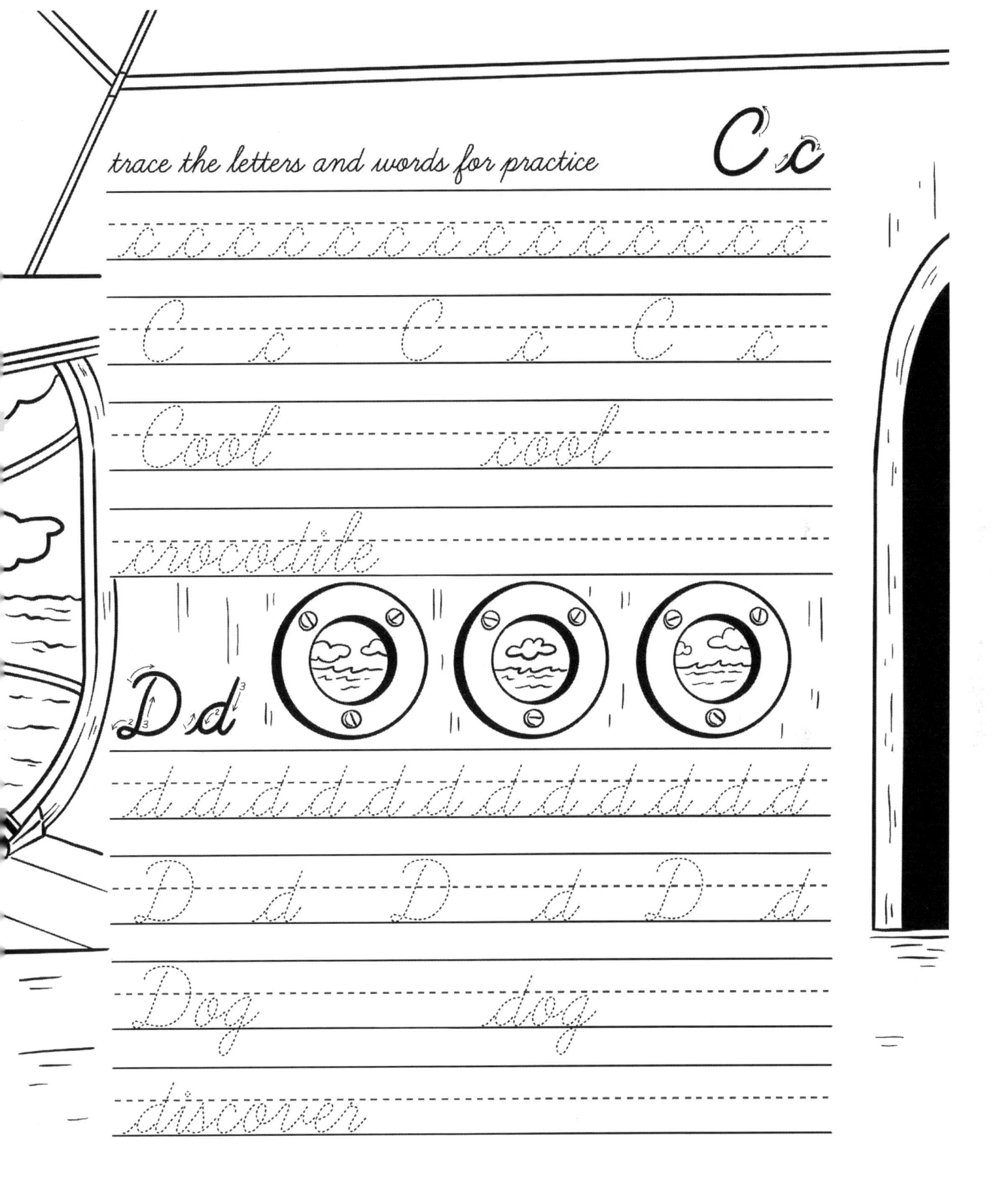

trace the letters and words for practice *Cc*

cccccccccccccccc

Cc Cc Cc

Cool   cool

crocodile

Dd

dddddddddddddd

Dd Dd Dd

Dog   dog

discover

Croc

dinghy

Dog

Practice!

Connectors

ca cb cc cd ce

cf cg ch ci cj

C

ck cl cm cn co

cp cq cr cs ct cu

cv cw cx cy cz

Practice!

Crack the Cursive Code — Connectors

da db dc dd de

df dg dh di dj

d

dk dl dm dn do

dp dq dr ds dt du

dv dw dx dy dz

trace the letters and words for practice. E e

e e e e e e e e e e e e e e e

E e   E e   E e

Eel   eel

electric

F f

f f f f f f f f f f

F f   F f   F f

Fox   fox

funny

Fox   Eel   fish

Practice!

CRACK the Cursive CODE — Connectors

ea eb ec ed ee

ef eg eh ei ej

e

ek el em en eo

ep eq er es et eu

ev ew ex ey ez

Practice!

CRACK the Cursive CODE — Connectors

f

fa fb fc fd fe

ff fg fh fi fj

fk fl fm fn fo

fp fq fr fs ft fu

fv fw fx fy fz

trace the letters and words for practice Gg

g g g g g g g g g g

G g G g G g

Gift gift

gorgeous

Hh

h h h h h h h h h h

H h H h H h

Hop hop

hound

Hammock   Goat   hook

Practice!

Crack the Cursive Code — Connectors

g

ga gb gc gd ge
gf gg gh gi gj
gk gl gm gn go
gp gq gr gs gt gu
gv gw gx gy gz

Practice!

CRACK the Cursive CODE — Connectors

h

ha hb hc hd he

hf hg hh hi hj

hk hl hm hn ho

hp hq hr hs ht hu

hv hw hx hy hz

trace the letters and words for practice. I i

i i i i i i i i i i i i i i i i i i i i

I i I i I i

Into into

incredible

J j

j j j j j j j j j j j j j j j j j j j j

J j J j J j

jump jump

journey

i i i i i i i i i i i

i i i i i

ii ii ii ii ii ii ii ii ii ii ii

ii ii ii ii ii

Jump

Island

jellyfish

j j j j j j j j j j j

j j j j j

jj jj jj jj jj jj jj jj jj jj

jj jj jj jj jj

Practice!

CRACK the Cursive CODE — Connectors

i

ia ib ic id ie

if ig ih ii ij

ik il im in io

ip iq ir is it iu

iv iw ix iy iz

Practice!

Crack the Cursive Code — Connectors

j

ja jb jc jd je
jf jg jh ji jj
jk jl jm jn jo
jp jq jr js jt ju
jv jw jx jy jz

trace the letters and words for practice.   K k

k k k k k k k k k k k

K k K k K k

kiss kiss

kooky

L l

l l l l l l l l l l l

L l L l L l

lazy lazy

lucky

K K K K K K K K K

K K K K K

k k k k k k k k k k k

k k k k k

Kite Leaves kennel

L L L L L L L L

L L L L L

l l l l l l l l l l l l

l l l l l

Practice!

CRACK the Cursive CODE *Connectors*

k

ka kb kc kd ke

kf kg kh ki kj

kk kl km kn ko

kp kq kr ks kt ku

kv kw kx ky kz

Practice!

CRACK the Cursive CODE Connectors

la lb lc ld le

lf lg lh li lj

l

lk ll lm ln lo

lp lq lr ls lt lu

lv lw lx ly lz

trace the letters and words for practice. **M m**

m m m m m m m m

M m M m M m

March march

marvelous

N n

n n n n n n n n

N n N n N n

Nose nose

navigate

Mountain   Necktie   map

Practice!

CRACK the Cursive CODE Connectors

ma mb mc md me

mf mg mh mi mj

m   *mk ml*

mm mn mo mp

mq mr ms mt mu

mv mw mx my mz

Practice!

CRACK the Cursive CODE — Connectors

na   nb   nc   nd   ne

nf   ng   nh   ni   nj

n   *nk   nl*

nm   nn   no   np

nq   nr   ns   nt   nu

nv   nw   nx   ny   nz

trace the letters and words for practice.   O o

o o o o o o o o o o o o o o o o o

O o   O o   O o

Over   over

outdoor

P p

p p p p p p p p p p

P p   P p   P p

Pals   pals

puzzled

Plant

Oasis

owl

Practice!

CRACK the Cursive CODE — Connectors

oa ob oc od oe

of og oh oi oj

O

ok ol om on oo

op oq or os ot ou

ov ow ox oy oz

Practice!

CRACK the Cursive CODE — Connectors

p

pa pb pc pd pe

pf pg ph pi pj

pk pl pm pn po

pp pq pr ps pt pu

pv pw px py pz

trace the letters and words for practice.   Qq

qqqqqqqqqqqqqqqqq

Q q Q q Q q

Quick   quick

question

Rr

nnnnnnnnnnnnnnn

R n R n R n

Rocky   rocky

riddle

Quail

Rainbow

rabbit

Practice!

CRACK the Cursive CODE — Connectors

q

qa qb qc qd qe

qf qg qh qi qj

qk ql qm qn qo

qp qq qr qs qt qu

qv qw qx qy qz

Practice!

CRACK the Cursive CODE *Connectors*

ra rb rc rd re

rf rg rh ri rj

r

rk rl rm rn ro

rp rq rr rs rt ru

rv rw rx ry rz

trace the letters and words for practice.

Ss

s s s s s s s s s s s s s s s

S s S s S s

Snake   snake

surprised

Tt

t t t t t t t t t t t t t t t

T t T t T t

Time   time

Twirled

Tree   Snake   scroll

Practice!

Crack the Cursive Code — Connectors

sa sb sc sd se

sf sg sh si sj

s

sk sl sm sn so

sp sq sr ss st su

sv sw sx sy sz

Practice!

Crack the Cursive Code — Connectors

t

ta tb tc td te

tf tg th ti tj

tk tl tm tn to

tp tq tr ts tt tu

tv tw tx ty tz

trace the letters and words for practice.   U u

u u u u u u u u u u u

U u U u U u

Up   up   Up

unison

V v

v v v v v v v v v v v

V v V v V v

Vivid   vivid

valuable

Volcano

Umbrella

vegetables

Practice!

CRACK the Cursive CODE — Connectors

ua ub uc ud ue

uf ug uh ui uj

u uk ul

um un uo up

uq ur us ut uu

uv uw ux uy uz

Practice!

CRACK the Cursive CODE — Connectors

ua   ub   uc   ud   ue

uf   ug   uh   ui   uj

u   *uk   ul*

um   un   uo   up

uq   ur   us   ut   uu

uv   uw   ux   uy   uz

trace the letters and words for practice W w

w w w w w w w w w

W w W w W w

Wings

wonderful

X x

x x x x x x x x x x

X x X x X x

extra

Xylophone

wand Xylophone Wings

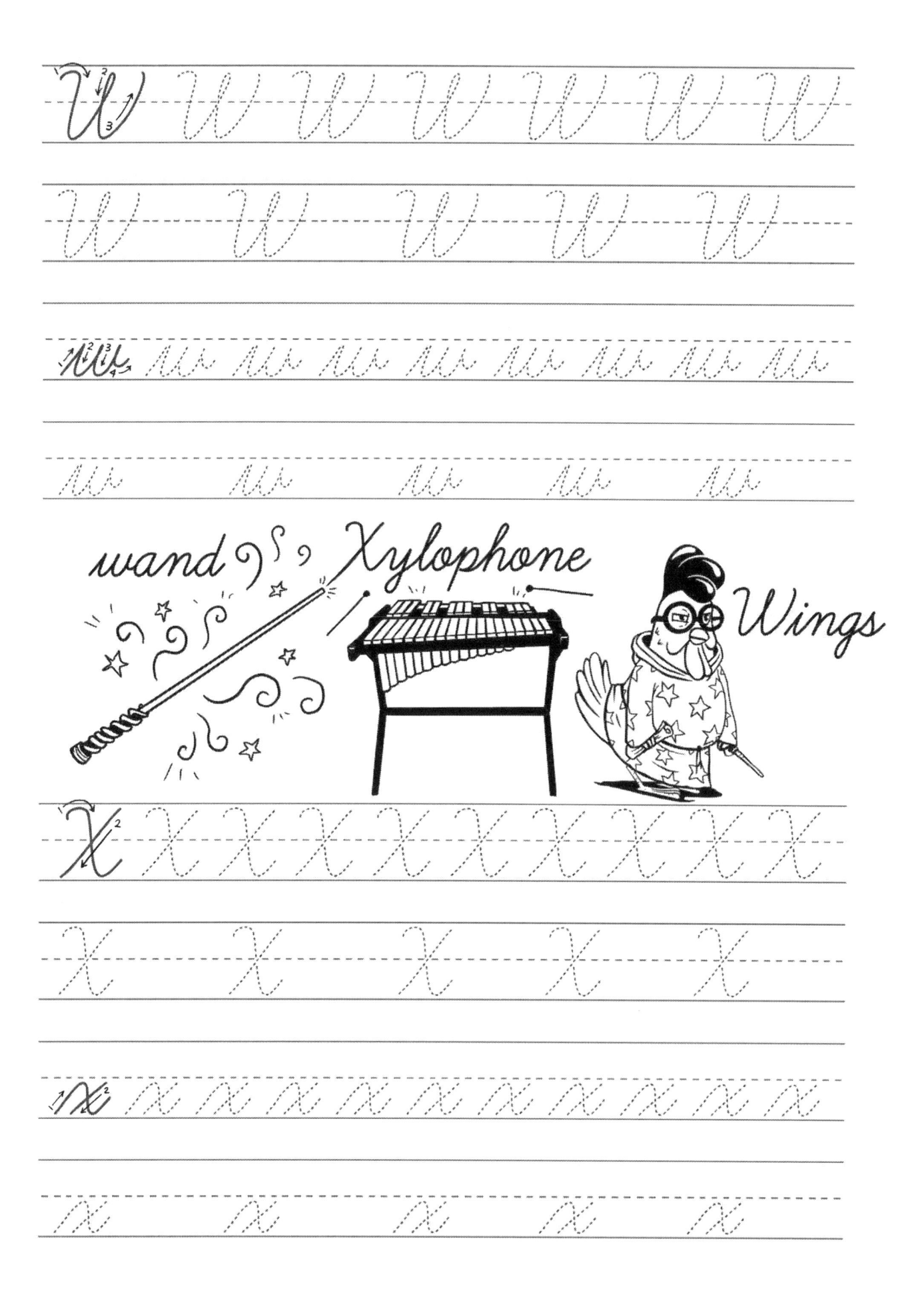

Practice!

CRACK the Cursive CODE — Connectors

wa ub wc wd we

wf wg wh wi wj

w wk wl

wm wn wo wp

wq wr ws wt wu

wv ww wx wy wz

Practice!

CRACK the Cursive CODE — Connectors

xa xb xc xd xe

xf xg xh xi xj

x

xk xl xm xn xo

xp xq xr xs xt xu

xv xw xx xy xz

trace the letters and words for practice. **Y y**

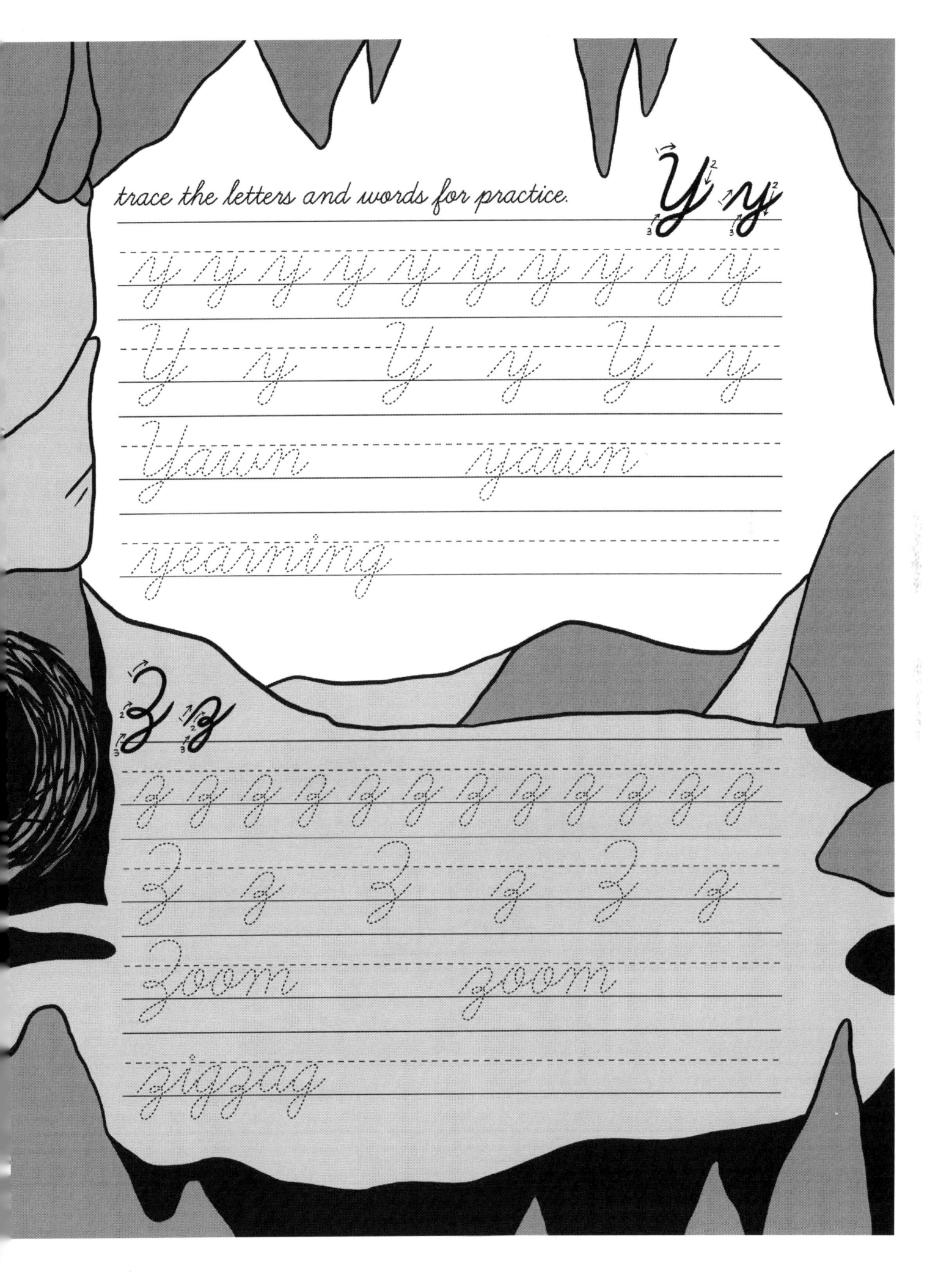

y y y y y y y y y y

Y y Y y Y y

Yawn yawn

yearning

Z z

z z z z z z z z z z

Z z Z z Z z

Zoom zoom

zigzag

Y y

Yarn Zipper yak

Z z

Practice!

CRACK the Cursive CODE — Connectors

Y

ya yb yc yd ye
yf yg yh yi yj
yk yl
ym yn yo yp
yq yr ys yt yu
yv yw yx yy yz

Practice!

CRACK the Cursive CODE — Connectors

z

za zb zc zd ze
zf zg zh zi zj
zk zl
zm zn zo zp
zq zr zs zt zu
zv zw zx zy zz

Practice!

The quick brown fox jumps over the lazy dog.

Practice

The quick brown

fox jumps over

the lazy dog.

The quick brown

fox jumps over

the lazy dog.

Practice!

The quick brown fox jumps over the lazy dog.

Practice

The quick brown

fox jumps over

the lazy dog.

The quick brown

fox jumps over

the lazy dog.

Practice!

The quick brown fox jumps over the lazy dog.

Practice!

The quick brown fox jumps over the lazy dog.

Practice!

Practice!

Practice!

Made in the USA
Columbia, SC
15 January 2025